My White dad, my Gay friend and my Black ass

a Personal Story

By

Larry A. Yff

TABLE of CONTENTS

<u>**INTRODUCTION**</u>

As a black man, should I hate my dad because he is white? I ask this because the media tells us statistically white men are responsible for American-style slavery, getting Donald Trump in office, high gas prices, low gas prices, Arby's, air and water pollution, corruption in the court system, the majority of serial-killing incidents, creating the dark web, most of the child sexual molesting cases, the slaughtering of Native Americans and a bunch of other horrible, weird and nasty shit.

I have a friend and he is gay. He is a *really* good friend and he is *really* gay. Can him and I really be friends since, based on my spiritual bellefs, I can't, don't and won't support or get involved in homosexual activity?

I am Black. Since my skin color is black, do I *have to* support all black people causes, not date white women and stand true to the belief that President Obama was a good President based on his skin color alone? Do I have to agree with everything the NAACP stands for?

I ask myself these questions and even answer them. Yes, this book is basically me talking to myself, questioning myself, answering myself and then telling all of you readers out there what me and myself have been thinking about.

I try to do all of that without sounding crazy, homophobic (even though that's not really a *thing*) or racist. Well, you bought the book, so let's get it started...

CHAPTER ONE

My White dad

My dad and mom are both white. There isn't anything spectacular, fascinating or original about that until you look at me: I am black.

Now that you know I am black, there are only a couple options to explain my situation. Instead of going through them all, I will give you the answer: I was adopted.

I was adopted by a white couple when I was about 1 week old. Ever since then, my life has been a roller coaster of emotions dealing with black and white issues. I've written a couple of books about it, with the main book being, "White, Confused, Black and Christian – the Autobiography of Larry A. Yff" (written in a base version and an explicit version), did several podcasts about it and now I am gonna go down a slightly different path with it.

White men get blamed for everything and maybe rightfully so. There are always at least 2 sides to every situation, so I think it's only fair to start there and a list is probably the best way to do that. I like lists and I'm not sure why I like them so much.

Now that I think about it, I won't do a list. I'm going to insert a Private Matter Bonus Essay called "White People Shit" to help me explain my dilemma a little better to you. Usually, these are a part of the Summary Section at the end of the book, but I'm going to give it to you here. Check it out:

Some White People Shit

SOME white guy invented basketball; ALL white people shouldn't try and take the credit for it.

SOME white people had black slaves; ALL white people shouldn't be blamed for it and labeled as prejudiced.

SOME white-boy cops are dicks and love to act big and bad in the hood because they used to get bullied; ALL white-boy cops aren't bad.

SOME white people came to America and made it what it is today; ALL white people should not be trying to claim it as their land.

SOME white people intentionally allowed cocaine to flood into black, urban America in the early 1980's; ALL white people shouldn't be blamed for it.

SOME white Christians swear up and down God, Jesus, the 12 disciples, the Virgin Mary and all the other important people in the Bible were white with long, blonde hair; ALL white Christians shouldn't be labeled as idiots and hypocrites.

SOME white people allowed American politics to become a shit-show full of drug use, cheating husbands, alcoholics, money-launderers, racism and any other type of corrupt and deceitful actions you can think of; ALL white politicians shouldn't be viewed like that. Well, actually, this one here's an exception.

The white guys who have been working the good ole' white boy system in American politics are either in on it directly or benefitting from it directly. So, in this case, and until America's current political system undergoes a major change...ALL white male politicians are considered by me to fall under that label.

SOME white people have hunted every wild animal on the planet into extinction; ALL white people shouldn't be blamed.

SOME white people are in secret labs mating lions with tigers and a bunch of other seriously gross and perverted shit; ALL white people shouldn't be considered gross and perverse.

SOME white people want to spend all their money trying to live on the moon or Mars or some other planet because they can't handle life on Earth; ALL white people shouldn't be labeled as intellectually sharp individuals with no people skills.

SOME white people do stupid shit…in the end ALL white people shouldn't be blamed for it.

So, what do you think? Here's my take on it. 1st off, I don't think it's fair to label all people with the same skin color a certain way. 2nd off, I don't think all people with the same skin color *are* a certain way and 3rd off, I don't think skin color has any real affect on a person's behavior. Let's tie this all in with my dad for a minute…

My dad, by classification, is a white male. That means, by classification, he is responsible for American-style slavery. Society has a way of labeling people by skin color to keep things simple. I fell into that societal norm and it got my brain all fucked up and messed up my side of my relationship with him…and that wasn't fair to him.

My dad has a genuine love and respect for me, he always has, but when I 1st became aware of the whole "white vs black" situation in America, I started to doubt his love for me. I drank the Kool Aid. I followed the hype. I listened to the media.

Based on the inputs and information I was getting from the media, world news and American society, I was learning there is a big difference between black and white people. I was being taught that skin color determines a person's value system, intelligence level, spirituality and ability to be an outstanding and productive member in society.

This message, as I dug a little deeper, was reinforced by American legislation: I found out about the Naturalization Act that stated "…only immigrants to America with white skin that come from

Europe and other countries that are classified as white, are allowed to gain American citizenship…"

This process didn't originate or start to solidify itself in my personal space until I graduated high school. At that point, I began to structure my life and my preferences around my skin color. I know I was talking about my dad, but I have to go on one more quick bunny trail and jump to another quick example to give you better insight, so stick with me here…

I was becoming a man. The world was telling me I wasn't becoming any man…I was becoming a black man. The world was telling me there is a clear, biological, natural difference between white men and black men.

In my life's journey to become a man, I found myself choosing a path: black man or white man. Because of my skin color alone, I couldn't be a white man, so by default, I had to live out my adult, male years as a black man. This meant I had to 1st figure out what in the fuck it means to be a black man as opposed to just being a man.

What I learned early on was it meant I, a black man, was somehow inferior to white men. It wasn't my intellect, the way I dressed, walked or talked that made me inferior…it was my skin color.

It had nothing to do with my experience, my likes, my dislikes, nothing…except my skin color.

My career possibilities were limited. If I wanted to pursue a field that was considered to be dominated by white men, it meant I had to somehow conform to white male behavior.

Sound confusing? You have no ideal!!! I once had thoughts about being in politics. I decided to pass because all I saw was white men were the only ones who were historically running and controlling all of the highest political offices in America. Why?

I had seen Republicans and Democrats argue about the stupidest shit and not reach a conclusion for months. I, as a black man, could clearly see an unbiased answer to the "major" dilemma they were facing. Why couldn't they see it? Why didn't their degrees and years of political cronyism allow them to see the blind simplicity in the answer?

As a black man, I was frustrated. I was frustrated because since my skin color was black, I somehow wasn't qualified to speak on such issues or be actively involved with them and I began to hate politics, at least American politics. I began to hate America. I began to hate white people. To be more specific: I began to hate white boys/men.

Why were white men allowed to run this country into the ground?

Why were white men allowed to pass legislation that was full of prejudice and remain in office?

Why were white men allowed to accept money from Big Business interests through corrupt lobbyists so that some white men would vote on legislation that hurt the American people's health…while making the Big Business owners wealthier?

It was a frustrating place to be. What made it more frustrating was when I would hear other black people, more specifically black men, tell me politics was for "those white boys." Black men in every circle of society I went through, either hated American politics and "those white boys" or were focused on creating black, political counterparts.

These counterparts were black lawyer associations and black political organizations such as the Congressional Black Caucus (CBC). The political system had become so crazy and white, that any group of people who weren't white had to also create their own congress within congress. I'm not sure, but I think there is a Latino Congressional Caucus and a couple other "inner-congresses".

This is a subject we will get into with more detail in the last chapter.

How does this relate to my dad? Since I now viewed myself as a black man, instead of as a man, I now began to view my dad as being my white dad. Do you see the shift? I allowed outside influences in my personal space and now I no longer had a dad and I was no longer a man.

Why did I begin to question my dad's love and intentions for me? I began to question it all based on his skin color: his skin was white.

Society needs to have a system that allows certain people to hold certain places in society. For instance, from the start, America decided only white people could be American citizens and that allowed white people (white men) who were interested in politics to dominate America's political landscape.

By making skin color a "thing", white people (white men) were able to have long, generational political ties and establish generations after generation of political power and influence. History shows us how, for centuries, white men used their political power and influence to 1) instill slavery, 2) classify black people as animals, 3) control housing and financial markets and 4) allow personal profit and gain to make decisions instead of voting based on common sense. I put my dad in that category, but I didn't put him there. Let me explain…

Remember, society tries to tell us if one white cop is bad…they're all bad. If one black man is a drug-dealer…they're all drug dealers. If one white, male politician is corrupt…they're all corrupt.

Enter my dad, Bob Yff. He, as a white American and as outlined by society is a bad person. Since the majority of corrupt politicians, crooked cops, racist judges, child-molesters and serial killers are white males…Bob Yff, in my eyes, was somehow a bad person.

But how? How can he be a bad person? He's my dad. He voluntarily adopted me. He grew up in the church and attends church faithfully. He has no kids outside of his 50-plus years of marriage to my mom. He has been an excellent provider for a household that included up to 7 kids at one time, all of who were not biologically his or his responsibility, making sure we stayed in the same house my entire childhood without getting evicted or having to move around. He never molested me. He never had me around women who weren't my mom.

So why did I doubt his love for me? How could I doubt his love for me? I doubted it because his skin was white. That's it and that's all. He has white skin.

That is a horrible way to judge somebody, but I fell for it. Who's to blame for the way I viewed my dad and pretty much all white men? Was it my fault for being ignorant and simple enough to be moved and persuaded by movies, television, news shows and society magazines?

I will openly confess and admit the answer to that question is "Yes." Yes, I am to blame…but in my view, only partially. And here's the part where, like I try to do with every chapter of every book I write, I tie it all with God somehow:

Whenever somebody commits a murder or does a crime, one of the 1st things investigators ask themselves, "Who gained the most from committing this crime?"

In a lot of murders, the person who is found guilty committed the crime for a very specific reason:

1. Somebody thought his neighbor was a child-molester and he didn't like child-molesters so he killed him. The benefit? He no longer had to live next door to a child-molester.

2. A man finds out his wife is cheating on him so he kills her and her lover. The benefit? His wife is no longer cheating.

In my investigative mind, I began to think: who benefits the most in society from all of this black versus white shit?

Do black people really benefit from having a Congressional Black Caucus? Do black people really benefit from having the "buy black" mentality? Do black people really benefit from protests against racist legislation and police brutality?

Do white people really benefit when they make racist legislation? Do white people really benefit from "whites only" hiring? Do white people really benefit from being involved in police brutality? Maybe my examples aren't the best, but we can still take a quick look at what I'm trying to get at...

When black people protest against a predominantly white police force or political office, what do they really gain? They sit there and march and protest and beg and plead and what really happens?

In the end, politicians will still vote the way they want to vote based on what they're familiar with.

They will still tend to vote based on who is giving them the most money unless...unless there is so much pressure from the public that in order to get votes or stay in office, the politician may succumb to the pressure and *promise* to act a certain way. Once he or she gets back in office, it tends to be business as usual and he or she will find a way to let the public know "his hands are tied and he's sorry he isn't able to fulfill his pre-election promise".

When black people get involved with "buy black", they are limiting their customer base. Since when did intentionally limiting your customer base become a good business tactic? We will touch on that more with the "My black ass" chapter

How about "whites only" hiring? A company who doesn't want to hire people based on talent is going to fall behind in whatever market they are in. Since when did intentionally limiting your talent pool become a good business tactic?

When a predominantly white political body passes legislation that is full of greed and prejudice, do they really benefit?

Alright, you knew this time would come, so don't act surprised: I'm about to tie this Chapter with God.

1st off, since there is no biological or scientific studies or evidence that can tie a person's IQ or ability to perform any general task, when people do things in attempt to gain a racial edge…you can never achieve your goal.

Since humans are scientifically one species, there can be no advantage to be gained for humanity when people with, for instance, white skin make laws or pursue agendas designed to give them a societal advantage over people with black skin.

Nothing is achieved other than causing a divide between humans and the more you divide a thing, the weaker you make it. I could give you the church as one of the best examples, but I won't. I already went down that path with the book, "Please Poke the Bear!: a Church Story".

Giving people with white skin an advantage hurts society as a whole because it concurrently gives other humans who have a different skin color a disadvantage. Intentionally trying to give other humans a disadvantage has no upsides for humanity and if that's what you're involved in, you're intentionally putting society and humanity at a disadvantage.

So, if people with white skin can't get a true advantage over people with black skin or vice versa, who benefits? Satan. Remember, this part of the Chapter is where I tie everything to spirituality...our unseen reality.

I believe there is a real being we call God who designed and created everything.

I believe God designed us to live in societies, create governments and rule over all other life forms on this planet in a responsible manner.

I believe there is a real being we call Satan who fell out of favor with God and was sent to Earth. I believe he hates the fact that us physical beings called humans are able to dominate and rule over him when he used to be a top being in the Kingdom of Heaven.

I believe it when the Lost Books of the Bible tell us Satan had a conversation with Adam and told him, "Since I fell out of favor with God, me and everyone who aligns themselves with me will do whatever it takes to make sure everything you do goes against God."

That means, I believe Satan and his allies are hard at work behind the scenes manipulating as many humans as they can into believing there is a superiority or advantage that can be gained over fellow humans based solely on skin color.

When society makes skin color a reason to kill each other, to take advantage of each other and to hate each other, I believe Satan and his allies are the main beneficiaries of that activity.

I will leave my beliefs at that. You have to find your own belief system and follow it...or not.

Here are my conclusions about this Chapter:

1. Learning to love a person past the color of their skin allowed me to have deeper, loving relationships

2. In my view, Satan is the main beneficiary of racial violence and intolerance

3. My dad loves me and he has white skin

4. I love my dad and I have black skin

5. I am a man and there is no biological or scientific difference or advantage between a man (or human) with black skin versus a man (or human) with white skin

6. Just because some white men act a certain way does not mean all white men act a certain way

Time to head to the next chapter and learn some shit about my views and experiences with love and homosexual activity...

CHAPTER TWO

<u>My Gay friend</u>

I have a friend who fits the label "Gay". I have to put those quotes around it because I don't use or like the term "Gay" as it refers to people. Here's my personal story about my "Gay" friend and why I want to share it with you. Check it out...

I was playing tennis with some friends one day. There was a guy with them I never met before. Him and I partnered up and I think we won. Him and I became cool from that day forward.

I knew he was in to homosexual activity so we had that conversation. It went something like this:

Me: "Hey. It was cool playing with you today. If you come here a lot, we can meet up and get some good exercise in. I am not into guys so as long as we keep that aspect cool, we can be tennis partners and friends."

Him: "No problem. I'm glad we started off on an honest tip and were able to talk about our differences and yeah, I'm cool with that."

From that day until today, we have been cool and good friends. Through the years we have kept in touch. I ask him questions about the part of his lifestyle that involves homosexual activity and he openly answers them.

I've asked him a lot of questions over the years because I am curious. Not membership-into-lgbt society curious...just curious. My curiosity with this segment of society increased as I began to 1) get closer to God and 2) reach the end of my addictions with coke/crack and pornos.

I had a double-curiosity because I have a big sister who lives in Texas who is also into homosexual activity and as I got closer to God, I got farther away from her. I wasn't comfortable supporting and participating in that lifestyle anymore but I still wanted to "have my big sister".

Between him and her, I pretty much was learning everything I needed to learn. You may be wondering why was I asking so many questions and why does it matter? Several reasons. Let's take a look at some of my main questions...

Question One: Can I be cool with a guy who is involved in homosexual activity? That was a serious question for me. I didn't mind being cool with people who had different sexual preferences than me, but I just wanted to know if no matter what he says, will there be some type of underlying physical attraction for me? Will he ever "accidentally" forget what we talked about one night, get drunk and try and cross the line in some form with me? Am I what people involved in homosexual activity call "homophobic"? Would I get in trouble if I killed him? Would that be taking it too far? These are all serious questions that ran through my mind.

They ran through my mind because there was so much confusion about what in the fuck Gay was and then there were Homos, Punks, Queers, Studs, Fish, Tops, Bottoms and a bunch of other terms the media was trying to tell us we all *had to* get familiar with and respect or be labeled as homophobic.

I didn't want to offend anybody based on their sexual preferences. My reason for this was hidden: I had begun to get a crazy porn-fetish for young girls!

I was what I considered normal, even though I was knee-deep in denial and a cocaine addiction that took every dollar I made. My porn addiction had taken me down a path that was embarrassing as shit! I was on a path that I couldn't share with anybody, because if I did, I would get labeled.

I would be labeled for my sexual preference and to me that wasn't fair. I was already being labeled for my drug addiction and I felt like shit. If I was to come clean about my cocaine-induced porn addiction (I only looked at porn when I was sniffing coke or smoking crack), the labels I would be called would be far worse than coke-head or crack-head.

I would be called a predator. A sexual deviant. A child-molester. A pedophile. I would be ranked lower than any addiction or social issue on the planet.

I think that's what made me sensitive to my gay friend. Let me stop right there for a minute. I don't like using the term "gay". Why am I labeling somebody by their sexual preference and why in the fuck would somebody want to wear that label?

I *definitely* didn't want to be labeled or characterized by my sexual tendencies! Similar to the addiction-related labels, I wanted no part of that and didn't want other people to go through what I was going through.

I was, by society's standard, a coke-head. I wasn't a man. I wasn't a human. I was simply a coke-head. That term eventually was down-graded to being a crack-head after I took my 1st hit of crack.

Since I didn't like the labels, it was my assumption my tennis partner didn't either, but he didn't care. His view was, "I'm a grown-ass man and I do whatever I want to do with my dick and if somebody don't like it, that's not my problem."

Taking on the labels of child-molester, freak, pervert and pedophile was not something I wanted to take on. To avoid that, I only shared my sexual thoughts, desires, likes and dislikes with people when I was high.

Since there was so much confusion, "homophobia" and shame associated with being involved in homosexual activity, I made it a point to stay in touch with my friend. I made it a point to do so at 1st to make a statement, I think.

My statement was that it was okay to have certain sexual

desires, preferences and needs that didn't agree with society. I was

taking the higher road and letting him and everybody else know that 1)

it wasn't cool to label someone based on sexual preference and 2)

regardless of your sexual taste, you were still a human.

I would go from having that view with him, to building an actual

friendship over time that had nothing to do with his or my sexual

preferences, so much so, that he was comfortable sharing stuff with

me and I shared with him.

I was out of State one time and visited him at his place. I went

out for the night and when I came back, he was on the living room

couch getting some "oral activity" from some dude.

I remember saying, "Hi" without a thought and went upstairs to

my room. I did something in my room and headed back downstairs,

through the living room, past the "oral action" to the kitchen. I made a

sandwich, a glass of juice or water and returned the way I came.

My point is, we were able to be friends without judging and I thought that was the way to be. I never called him or anyone else involved in homosexual activity Gay. I didn't call them Punks, Queers or any of those terms.

I was surprised, as the lgbt community picked up steam over the years, that people *wanted* to be labeled as Queer, Gay or as Punks. When I was growing up, those terms were all rude and disrespectful. All the labels and acceptance of it added confusion to my life. The confusion would be heightened as I got closer to one of my big sisters.

I would often times go down to her State and live with her. She had a same-sex/homosexual "wife". Do you see how hard it is to talk with all of the new and old terms? Anyways...

I was comfortable with her and her sexual lifestyle just like I was with my tennis friend until...until I began to get close with God. As I began to get a better understanding of Him, I began to realize I was disrespecting Him. I had to make a choice.

So, with my sister, I would attend homosexual events and clubs with her. I didn't care because I was never scared or disliked people involved in homosexual activity...I was just confused.

I was confused as to why 2 dudes would want to have sex with each other in the butt rather than be with a female.

I was confused why a man would try and tuck his dick between his legs with tap (I think), try and walk like he had hips like a female and try and talk "like a female".

I was confused why a female wouldn't want to have sex with a man, but she did want to have her female partner strap-on a fake dick and have sex with her.

I was confused as to how a female could say she wanted to be with another woman...but she had 3 kids by her previously partner/boyfriend.

Until I got close to God, none of this really mattered. It did leave me confused, but not confused enough to start judging people...not yet.

I remember going to a club my sister managed and we met a homosexual couple. The "female" girl liked my sister because she was what was considered a Stud. A Stud is the female who wants to appear to be more masculine and take on the man/provider/protector role in the house that a husband would typically fill. Anyways...

I wound up having sex with the "female" girl's Stud. That caused more confusion...but not enough for me to not have sex with her. I couldn't understand how she, as an attractive female with a nice body, wanted to deny her obvious, feminine traits and characteristics and be the "man" in her relationship, but be the woman that she was when her and I had sex.

I had sex with a lot of studs actually. They were females and they had vaginas that wanted to occasionally have a dick or 2 up inside them. So why were they acting and dressing like men? More confusion.

My big sister and I would eventually part ways, but it had nothing to do with her sexual orientation. It had more to do with my addictions and the crazy part was, she always accepted me and my addictions and the crazy sex shit I like and even my frequent cocaine binges where I would watch porn for 48 hours straight without blinking.

The crazy thing was, my tennis friend and my big sister both had no problem with my sexual preferences or my addictions...but here I was, about to turn the corner in my faith, about to start judging them and myself with a different yardstick.

Before you think I was only focused on homosexual activity as being the only sexual sin God cares about, I need you to know I was also involved with committing adultery. I wasn't cheating on my wife...I was cheating with someone else's wife.

My sister was well aware of it, but she still didn't judge me. Her view was that if I was okay with it, then she was okay with it. All of this sexual acceptance kept everybody comfortable in our family and friend relationships.

Having no judgement was a comfortable place for everybody involved. We were all free to do what we liked as long as we liked it. We were able to be friends and family and enjoy life until, like I said, I got serious about God and this is the part you knew was coming.

You knew I was gonna tie it all into God somehow because that's what I do with every chapter in every book. If this is the 1st book of mine that you have read, you still should know what's about to come next because I just tied God into the last chapter *and* I told you that's how I get done.

Alright, enough stalling. I was giving those of you who don't want to hear about God, especially as it relates to homosexual activity, to check out, skip this part and move on to the next chapter for some more personal information. Are you still here? Good. Let's get into some God stuff mixed with homosexual activity…

When I turned the corner and started to live my life according to God and His laws, I began to view things differently. The 1st thing I began differently relating to sex was my view on pornography. Wait. This chapter is about homosexual activity and my friend and I don't want to get off track by talking about my personal sexual-preference change and get everybody confused.

However, when my view did change, based on the guidelines God gave humanity through the Bible and the Lost Books of the Bible, I had to start questioning my relationships, both with family and with friends.

Since I believed I God created everything we see and don't see, I believed He deserved my respect and honor by following His laws. Because of that, I had to begin to rethink the areas in my life that were the most damaging. Sex and drugs were at the top of my list.

I was having sex outside of marriage (against God's law) and it was resulting in several kids out of wedlock, rendering me a dead-beat and absentee father. Not good.

I was lusting (against God's law) by watching pornos and it was taking me down a dark path. I was heading down a path that made me fantasize about having sex with young girls and a bunch of other fetish stuff. Porn addiction via lust was basically giving me ED.

For those of you unfamiliar with this term, it stands for Erectile Disfunction. Still doesn't ring a bell? Basically, it means your dick can't get hard and that means it is not erect and that means your dick is un-functionable.

I became sexually dysfunctional because my lust and taste for pornography trapped me deep in a sexual fantasy world. I couldn't operate in the real world sexually at all. That was me, but enough about me...

I now had to start looking at all of God's laws surrounding sex and decided to address them all. I already told you I had an unnecessary "soft spot" for people with what I called sexual disorders like myself, because of my personal experiences.

I was molested one time when I was between 4 and 7, so after analyzing and dealing with that aspect of my young sexual encounters, I also had to "give child molesters" a pass.

I gave them a pass because my porn addiction, even though it hadn't manifested itself in the real world, had me heading towards being a potential molester and pedophile and put me in the frame of mind of, "If I can't find compassion for someone like that…I can't expect to receive compassion for myself and my sexual ways."

For some reason, I now put homosexual activity in that same boat. I was hearing some people say they were born that way; while others said they only went that route because they had been sexually-molested as a child and often for years. Either way, I wanted to make sure I treated them like anybody else because we all "have our flaws".

I began to view homosexual activity as the sin that it is and I was willing to view that sexually sinning person exactly as I viewed my sexually sinning ass. But there was a problem: the Bible.

It seemed as though people involved with homosexual were all very willing to give God the middle-finger. The response I got, after talking with my friend who is involved in homosexual activity regarding the Bible was:

1. The Bible talks about other sexual sins besides homosexuality, so if you want the truth, people are hypocritical for picking and choosing which sexual sins to attack, so for that reason…I don't care what God or the Bible say about homosexual activity.

2. The Bible has been manipulated so much that we can't say for sure whether or not God really said what the Bible says it does,

so for that reason…I don't care what God or the Bible say about homosexual activity.

3. I just let people do what they want. God gave everybody the freedom to do whatever they want, so why would He condemn somebody for wanting to be involved in Gay activity? Since God gave us a choice…I don't care what God or the Bible say about homosexual activity.

There is the conversation in a nutshell. Since he knows I am taking a stand against homosexual activity based on the Bible, he took the position of saying he respected God, but since he wasn't sure what parts of the Bible were or were not true, he made a conscious decision to do his own thing and let the chips fall where they may.

My friend is gay. He doesn't view God or the Bible like I do and he has no intention of changing. Can we still be friends? Should I take the holier-than-thou road and tell him we need to cancel our friendship?

I posed that question to my gay friend and he said it would sadden him if I decided to part ways, but life would go on.

Is it right for me to give him that ultimatum? Can I be friends with someone who blatantly disrespects God? What about my big sister in Texas who is into homosexual activity? Should I present her with the same ultimatum?

They both have accepted me and all my bullshit. Now that I have decided to take a position in life that goes against their lifestyle, would I be wrong to cut ties?

The topic of homosexuality and Christianity, when I stop and think about it, has presented me with a lot of questions I don't have answers for. In the same vein, it has presented me with a lot of answers that I don't need to question.

In the end, I have decided:

1. Because I was lost in sexual sin and had a change of direction and decide to take a stand against sexual sin does not make me a hypocrite. It makes me smarter and wiser. A hypocrite is a person who says one thing and does another…not a person who used to do a certain activity, learned a new way of doing that thing differently to better his life and decided to take a stand against his past activity (as long as he isn't still involved in doing it the old way).

2. I will not support homosexual activity in any way shape or form and I take that stance against as many of the list of sexual sins God presented us with as I can.

3. I will not get involved In debates and arguments about the relevance of the Bible as it relates to homosexual activity. The Bible is a very, historically accurate representation of God's interaction with humans and His intentions for sexual activity. I will not waiver from God's view to appease anybody's choice.

4. My sister will always be my sister, just like I will always be her
brother. My "gay" friend will still be my friend even though our
views on God and the Bible may be different.

I have touched on a couple of issues in the previous 2 chapters
that will be discussed in the next chapter BUT I add a little somethin'
somethin' to it. So, if you start to come across some subject matter
that you think we already went through, remember what I just told
you and keep reading…

CHAPTER THREE

<u>My Black ass</u>

I would like to take the time to use this Chapter and tell you some personal, random things about Larry. Who is Larry and why should I listen to *his* black ass? Well, I'm going to give you a couple of reasons and I'm thinking you will be able to get through all of the rambling, drawn-out sentences, cuss-words and all the riff-raff to find yourself at least one reason to pay attention to some of the words I have laid out on paper for you. Let's see…

My black ass can *definitely* share with you a thing or two about marriage, drug addiction, porn addiction, violence, inter-racial adoption, being an absentee father and last but not least…about the importance of getting in touch with God. Seriously. People underestimate the God aspect, and in my view, that is the main thing that doesn't allow people to get over the humps and hurdles life can present.

I got married 12/20/2020. I like saying that date and writing that date down because it looks cool. It's like the perfect date. It's also like the perfect mix of lottery numbers to play and all that stuff is about the only perfect stuff in a marriage, well at least in my marriage.

That day had to be one the calmest, beautiful-est, relaxing-est, peaceful-est days of my life. I knew I loved Netta Ruth and I knew I wanted to marry her...I just didn't necessarily know it would be that soon.

We knew each other off and on for several years prior to getting married. It wasn't until I moved to Muskegon Michigan that we would actually live in the same city, share the same house, seal the deal and get married.

That process of moving to Muskegon and all the other stuff took about two and a half months. When we decided to pull the trigger and get married, we had already been through several rough patches because of me.

A month before I moved to Muskegon, she came to visit me in Grand Rapids and I was high as a giraffe on crack. By that, I mean I was high…not the giraffe.

When I got to Muskegon, we made at least 2 plans to see each other and I had to cancel them both because I was high on crack (I won't use the giraffe illustration because I think it confused some of you. I think some of you were like, "A giraffe on crack? That's a horrible example. Giraffes don't smoke crack!" Anyways…).

My point is, I had admitted to myself and a couple of other select individuals about how crazy my life had become as an addict, but I hadn't let her or people at the church we both attended know my situation.

Even after witnessing my crazy 1st-hand, she still was down to get married. She said she was able to use her spiritual eyes to see past my addiction and understand my pain.

We were both deep into getting personal with God and we decided, even after all the madness, that if we are gonna do this thing, we better do it now. She was basically telling me she wanted to get married, but if she saw too much more of my crazy…she may change her mind.

I pushed the date ahead as fast as possible, giving her as little time as possible to change her mind. We got married at a church we had never been to before and my life has never been the same.

Here's where I can go through some aspects of marriage that some of you may have experienced either in marriage or being in a committed relationship. Sharing these couple of experiences should give you a couple of wedding/marriage tips. Let's see…

1. **I'm married…not blind**. Once you get married, it doesn't mean you will never see another attractive person in your life. You will continue to see them. The key to a successful marriage is what you do with the images you will undoubtedly see. I am

completely turned on by Netta. She has the body-type I like.

I'm what you would call an "ass man" and she has that. She

also has the titty size I like. I'm more in the middle when it

comes to these. I don't need watermelons…but I also need

more than a golf ball. Somewhere between a Granny Smith

apple and a cantaloupe is about right for me. I guess if I was

gonna stick with my fruit analogies, a pomegranate would sum

it up the best. I also love her hands, legs, teeth, forehead,

eyes, hips, feet, elbows, lips… Even with that complete,

physical package, it does not mean throughout the day I won't

come across an attractive female. I come across the same

amount of them I came across pre-marriage. That hasn't

changed. My view on them is what changed. As a married

man, I allow myself the opportunity to acknowledge a female's

beauty or attractiveness and ask myself a couple of questions.

One question is, "What could I gain by engaging in a

conversation with her?" As I fast-forward our conversation in my mind, I realize I have nothing to gain but some good conversation and a whole lot to lose and that is my marriage. My wife and I are supposed to be able to trust each other. If I allow myself to randomly spark up conversations, I will not have to try and hide texts or delete them or put her name in my cellphone under "Scam Likely" or a bunch of other sneaky shit and I don't have the time for all of that...so I don't have those conversations. I also ask myself, "What if I did get past the conversation stage? What would the best outcome be?" Typically, the best outcome I arrive at would be sex. I could get a random shot of ass but if I got caught, my black ass could get another random shot...and it wouldn't be ass! It would be from a gun my loving, beautiful wife would purchase. That's the thought process I allowed myself to go through in the beginning of my marriage. Now, with about 18 months under my belt, I don't even have to fast-forward the scenario that far. I simply understand my best and worst-case scenarios and understand them clearly and can make the easy decision to acknowledge…and move the fuck on!

2. **Who am I accountable to in a marriage?** I can honestly say my marriage has made it through a lot of dumb shit because I know I am not accountable to my wife 1st. I am accountable to God. He is the one who laid out the rules, laws and regulations of what marriage is for us humans. If I were to step outside my marriage, yes, I would be breaking a contract with Netta, but I would also be breaking a contract I made in front of and to God. There is only so much she can do to me as opposed to all of the stuff God could put on me. I would much rather take an "accidental" bullet from her for cheating, If that were to happen, than to take what God could give me for disrespecting marriage. I live by the code Jesus told us when He said, "Fear no man. A man can only kill your body. You need to fear the One who can kill your body AND your soul."

3. **Her and I make up the foundation for all personal, spiritual and financial quests.** That's just a fancy way of saying marriage is all about her and me. We come 1st. There is no "we" in team, but when you team up with a partner in marriage, there is no time to live it by a cliché. There were some awkward moments in realizing the reality of this point. This meant, none of the children she brought to the table nor any of the children I bring to the table hold priority over our team. One of my daughters was in the car with us and shared her soul. She talked about how she felt like I didn't have any time for her since I got married. She felt as though I was taking all my time with Netta and my "new family" and it didn't feel good. That hurt me to my core! If I could figure out some way to show a pause while I'm writing and find some way to cry on paper…now would be that time. She was crying as she expressed herself. Since I was confident and secure in my stance that Netta and me are a team with a destiny and we are

accountable to God 1st, I was able to keep calm and make that a learning moment for everyone in the car. I explained to her that she will always be my daughter. That will NEVER change. We then explained to her that Netta will always be the Number One female in my life and that is over my mothers, daughters or nieces. Netta will never lose her position as wife and my daughter will never lose her position as daughter. To sum it up: Netta and I understand that in order for this marriage thing to work, we had to find the "we" in team and make sure we keep that in the forefront of every decision we make.

4. **Marriage is sacred and for a man and a woman.** Once we chose to follow God's laws, we no longer had to get involved in conversations about homosexual marriage. We didn't have to argue about the legality of it in Michigan versus the legality of it in some of State or Country. We didn't give a fuck what any manmade law said on it: we follow God's law. End of story

with no discussion or debate. When one of her sisters, who is involved in a homosexual relationship, was about to get married, Netta chose to stay out of it and not allow her kids to be a part of it. She had to make a choice to go with God's will or her sister's choice. She chose God. It wasn't easy, but it was an opportunity to show both her love for God and her love for family: she will always have love for her sister, but that love will have boundaries. The boundary in this situation was they were still sisters and still loved each other and she still has a love and respect for the female her sister married, but Netta can't support any type of activity that goes against God's laws. In this case it related to God's definition of what marriage is. I talked about my situation with my big sister who has lived the homosexual lifestyle for years and how it started to affect me and my view on our relationship. I had to make sure I loved her as a person, just like she loved me as a person BUT I also had to be prepared to not support any type of homosexual activity like in the case of her getting married. I wouldn't be able to attend. At 1st, this was a hard concept to wrap my noodle around because she supported me through my sexual sins of lusting and committing adultery and now here I was, a changed man saying I couldn't do the same for her? I guess that's where you have to be bold. You have to take a stand. You can either continue to sin or support others in sin or you can learn a new way, turn from sin and support others in a different way. A way that gives God his respect and honor. It gets tricky, trust me. My advice is to take the emotion out of it and focus on God. "Seek 1st the Kingdom of God…" As I focus on the big picture, I am able to see through the snapshots of sin I will approach in life.

Choosing to follow God's laws hasn't been an easy thing. It has made people call me a hypocrite. For some reason, that's been the most common go-to for people who are involved in activities that go against God's laws; especially when the advice is coming from my black ass!

I've had people ask me, "Larry, how can you talk about not doing drugs and a bunch of other shit when you used to do stuff? You're being a hypocrite!"

Actually, I'm not a hypocrite, like I stated earlier. What I am is smart. I have learned from my past experiences a better way to live life and feel a God-given responsibility to share both sides of the coin with as many people as want to pay attention.

I would be a hypocrite only if I was telling everybody about how they should change their ways like I did...if I was still dippin' in and out of the shit I was telling *them* not to do. THAT is being a hypocrite or hypocritical.

Alright, we touched on addiction, marriage, kids...what else do I think I could share with you that could make a difference? I got it! Check this out...

I love being open and honest. That has to be one of the best cures for depression and suicidal thoughts, well, kind of…

When my black ass decided to actively and intentionally live a life based on God's laws, it meant I had to 1st get real with myself. Part of that process meant accepting the fact I was a crackhead. Now, I said being open is a good cure…but I didn't say that shit wouldn't be painful.

Do you realize how much deeper my black ass went into depression after I said that shit out loud? Going down the path I had chosen to go down meant you had to, like Jesus shared with us, "…1st get the log out of your eye, *then* help others get the sliver out of theirs.

Part of this process for me meant having to do a whole lot of admitting to a whole lot of nasty, stupid, repetitive, ignorant, retarded, crazy, explicit, dirty, deranged shit! But I did it and I would encourage all of you to do it. It helps. It may not feel too good at 1st but at later it will…or at least it should.

If you can't admit and face your own problems, how are you ever going to be able to help other people with their problems? That question right there leads me to talk about the church for a second.

The church is supposed to be a place where people who are interested in spiritual matters can go. It's supposed to be a place of enlightenment. The church is supposed to be a place where anyone who is interested in making some serious changes in their lives can turn to...but it's not and here's where I think the church body has fallen short.

I had a problem with cocaine addiction. I approached 2 different churches to get that 1st step towards recovery with God that I was looking for. When I walked in one church and asked to speak to an elder about it, they looked at me like I wasn't supposed to be there, 1st off and 2nd off, they looked confused.

I repeated what I was looking for and an elder and some other church member and myself held hands, they did a prayer for my recovery and told me they hoped things would get better.

There was no connecting me with somebody in the church who had similar problems. There was no type of additional steps past their prayer for me. I went to another church.

This church, I knew the pastor personally. After telling him what I was looking for, he basically told me I needed to get my shit together and if I was able to do that, he would love to have me be some type of contributing member to the church.

My point is, I believe if churches are supposed to be a sanctuary and guide for healing, they need to have a contact list ON HAND, so that they can steer anyone coming to them for help in the right direction. I also believe this should involve some type of continuous follow-up effort on the side of the church.

I could go all day long about my views on the church, but I gotta keep going. I'm gonna hit as many different topics I can to try and reach somebody so I can teach somebody about some of the life-changing shit I've gone through. Moving on…

As I chose to live a life according to God, people started to call me angry…and they were right! I would see things and get mad as shit!

I couldn't watch movies anymore that depicted the bad guys as being super powerful, aggressive, handsome and bold; while they showed angels as being weak and gentle. It made me mad! It made me send Jesus a personal request to allow me to take over the media! Let me control the movie industry that insists on making sure homosexual activity is viewed as being normal and okay! Let me control the millions of commercials that bombard us every day promoting alcohol consumption and the use of "legal" pills! I would eliminate a lot of that shit and run it according to God's laws and standards.

I couldn't listen to gospel songs anymore that talked about "God opening the doors of Heaven and pouring out blessings on you" because they didn't include a verse that explains why God would do that. The songs didn't talk about what you had to do *before* God was obligated to bless you! It made me mad! It made me send Jesus a personal request to allow me to take over the gospel music industry, the secular music industry and the entire church body! I would run it according to God's laws.

I would see in the news how wealthy people would never go to jail. They could steal billions of dollars and destroy millions of people's lives…and never see a day in jail. It made me mad! It made me send Jesus a personal request to take over the entire judicial system, starting with America, and then affecting the world's system of justice! I would run it all by God's laws.

I would see wealthy developers try and show a personal interest in a physically, run-down area…only to try and get approval and sympathetic tax breaks so they can buy all the property and make millions of dollars while saying, "Fuck you!" to the current residents! I made me send Jesus a personal request that would make me the largest land-holder on the planet! I would control it and run it according to God's laws!

Man! I just got myself physically worked up, agitated, excited and angry all at once! I better hurry up and switch gears before I get that "angry, black man" label.

Speaking of "black man" label. I will only hit this point lightly about purchasing power. I don't think it's right for black people to try and take the approach of "buying black".

I understand the emotional backing behind that train of thought, but it's counter-business. It hurts black-owned business bottom lines and does something it is trying to go against: puts one group of people with a certain skin color over another. In my view,

that isn't a good thing and I don't and won't participate in it.

In that same vein, I don't feel the need to participate in any

agenda that is based on skin color. I see the need for a Mexican-

American Caucus and a Congressional Black Caucus and what other

political groups out there that are forming…but I think in the end, their

objectives will not be met. I think they will be counter-productive

because the goal should not be to make all skin colors equal…it should

be to promote God's agenda for all humanity regardless of the non-

factor of skin color. Let's hit one more topic, shall we?

Actually, I think I've thrown enough at you to take a look at

about my black ass. If you want to know more about me and my

views, there are at least 30 other books in my series that shed more

light on more areas. I don't want to spoil them for you by repeating

myself here.

<u>**SUMMARY and Private Matter Bonus Essays**</u>

I've said a lot about a lot in this book. I'm actually a little emotionally drained from it. Whatever I haven't already said will probably be covered in one of the Private Matter Bonus Essays or one of the other books in my "Your View Matter" series.

Thanks for reading!!!

And that's all I have for a summary. Take a look at the next section that is full of some short essays. These essays are me sharing my views on things we talked about in this book:

Some White People Shit

SOME white guy invented basketball; ALL white people shouldn't try and take the credit for it.

SOME white people had black slaves; ALL white people shouldn't be blamed for it and labeled as prejudiced.

SOME white-boy cops are dicks and love to act big and bad in the hood because they used to get bullied; ALL white-boy cops aren't bad.

SOME white people came to America and made it what it is today; ALL white people should not be trying to claim it as their land.

SOME white people intentionally allowed cocaine to flood into black, urban America in the early 1980's; ALL white people shouldn't be blamed for it.

SOME white Christians swear up and down God, Jesus, the 12 disciples, the Virgin Mary and all the other important people in the Bible were white with long, blonde hair; ALL white Christians shouldn't be labeled as idiots and hypocrites.

SOME white people allowed American politics to become a shit-show full of drug use, cheating husbands, alcoholics, money-launderers, racism and any other type of corrupt and deceitful actions you can think of; ALL white politicians shouldn't be viewed like that. Well, actually, this one here's an exception. The white guys who have been working the good ole' white boy system in American politics are either in on it directly or benefitting from it directly. So, in this case, and until America's current political system undergoes a major change...ALL white male politicians are considered by me to fall under that label.

SOME white people have hunted every wild animal on the planet into extinction; ALL white people shouldn't be blamed.

SOME white people are in secret labs mating lions with tigers and a bunch of other seriously gross and perverted shit; ALL white people shouldn't be considered gross and perverse.

SOME white people want to spend all their money trying to live on the moon or Mars or some other planet because they can't handle life on Earth; ALL white people shouldn't be labeled as intellectually sharp individuals with no people skills.

SOME white people do stupid shit...in the end ALL white people shouldn't be blamed for it.

HOMOSEXUAL ACTIVITY

I am against homosexual activity. Not because I don't like it. Not because I think it's weird. Not because I don't understand it...I am against homosexual activity because it goes against God's laws.

To be clear and fair, homosexual activity is only one of God's laws regarding sex that I am against. This may sound hypocritical, and people who are involved in homosexual activity or people who are against God, love to say that, but yes, I used to break all kinds of God's laws on sex.

God said we aren't supposed to cheat on our husbands or wives...I slept with a couple of married women in my day. That was wrong only because it went against God's laws and I had to stop. Did I want to stop? Not really, but I had no choice: it was either follow God's laws or my own laws.

God said we aren't supposed to lust. That means we aren't supposed to allow ourselves to see someone and view them as a piece of meat. I used to deal with that when I had a major porn addiction.

I would get high and watch porn for hours until my eyeballs dried up. I loved it. The rush of the endorphin releasing drug with the rush of the porn-visual had me hooked for years. I had to stop doing it. Did I want to stop? Not really, but I had no choice: it was either follow God's laws or my own laws.

People, particularly in the church, who love to point out the wrongs of homosexual activity, tend to forget about God's other laws surrounding sex. They like to point out homosexual activity while they themselves are lusting at strip clubs, hooked on porn or phone sex, cheating on their husband or wife or having sex with a very, very close family member.

This topic has been beaten up a lot and blown out of proportion. At this stage in the game, I understand 99% of humans are not involved in homosexual activity and 99% of humans don't understand homosexual activity and 99% of humans are scared to speak up and state their view because of media, personal, professional and social backlash.

I am not concerned with any of that, so I can speak freely. I follow God's laws as best as I can and I know He designed this place and that He runs shit, to if anybody has a problem with me stating my views...oh well. Get over it because I'm not stating my views, I'm stating God's views.

Anything I've done in the past that went against God's laws is something I have both an obligation to stop doing, openly confess what it is I was doing AND help people who are interested in following God's laws to stop as well. While we're on the homosexual subject, let's also be clear:

1. there is no such thing as homophobia or homophobic. People aren't scared of people who are involved in homosexual activity.

That's a very effective term that people involved in homosexual

activity have used to get their "opponents" to shut the fuck up,

back down and let homosexual activity become a normal thing

in society.

2. I don't call people involved in homosexual "homosexuals, gay,

    questioning, queer, bi-sexual, lesbian, stud, dike, fish, top or

    bottom" or whatever other labels are out there. I refuse to

    characterize someone by their sexual choices and preferences.

    If you like homosexual activity, you are simply a man or woman

    who likes homosexual activity.

3. I am not changing my basic understanding of the English

    language and start calling people "him/her/she/he." That's

    about the stupidest, dumbest thing I could ever do. It's not that

    I don't respect everyone's freedom of choice…it's simply

    because I know how to speak English and I know that "he" is a

    pronoun that describes a single, individual male. There is

    enough changing of the English language with words like "bad", "shit" and "lit" meaning a thousand different things. I sure as fuck am not about to start calling "him" a "her" and "she" a "he" or "me" a "him/her/he/she."

4. Any State or country can legalize homosexual marriage, and any human who follows God's laws cannot give a shit. I guess if a State says humans can marry animals that I, as a business owner, would have to start allowing spousal support for a German Shepherd's husband or wife that is an employee of mine? Get the fuck out of here. Won't happen. I operate along God's laws and am under His government's protection, guidance and care, so make whatever laws you want: if they go directly against God's laws, I will never follow them and you will never force me to.

In the end, do whatever *you* want. Suck on whoever *you* want. Fuck whoever *you* want. Marry whoever *you* want. Use fake dicks when *you* have fake sex if *you* want. Buy a fake vagina and have fake titties if *you* want...do whatever *you* want if *you* want to follow *your* own rules. When you want to wake up like I had to do and start following God's nice and easy rules for sex…let me know. I had to learn the hard way, but I might be able to help you switch over…if that's what you want.

BLACK AND PETTY

When I see a police-officer parked in a parking lot trying to be sneaky and catch somebody speeding or setting a speed trap on the highway, I speed up so I'm going at least 10 miles over the speed limit in his face. Why? Because I hate what police officers stand for and how they universally in America have, and continue to have a horrible reputation and track record with black people...and because I'm black and petty.

When I come to a stop sign, I don't do a complete stop. Why? Because I hate what American laws are and how prejudicial they are so if I do a complete stop like I'm supposed to, it means I'm complying with American laws and I don't want to recognize and follow any law system that was geared towards killing and targeting black people...and because I'm black and petty.

When I walk across the street I jay-walk. Why? Once again, America's laws were established to *protect* white people from black people and to give white people whatever edge they could over black people whether it be financial, economic, religious, educational, political or in the area of business and since jaywalking is a law made by white people, I'm not going to adhere to it. That and the fact that I'm black and petty.

I have guns even though I'm technically not supposed to. Why? Since American gun laws allowed white civilian, military and police officers to use their guns to shoot and kill black men without ever seeing a day in jail, I'm not going to abide by *their* unequal gun laws…and I'm black and petty.

When election time rolls around, I don't vote. Why? American politics have a horrible history of manipulating voting districts and finding as many ways as possible to not allow black people to participate equally in the voting system.

Also, politicians can declare war and not have their kids go to war.

Also, American politics is totally corrupted by big business, racial bias and money so there's not really going to be a difference as to who's in office if everybody has their hands tied by money, the good ole' white boy system and ass-grabbing, so why vote? Also, for the last 400 years, I have a choice to vote between two old ass white men to lead my country as President. That's not really a choice, so that's another big reason why I don't vote. I also don't vote because I'm black and petty.

I don't like going to white churches. Why? White churches and Christianity have tried to teach us that Jesus, all the angels, God and all the prophets were all white guys with blonde hair and blue eyes. Since history, science, the Bible and basic geography show us Jesus and the rest of them *definitely* were not white, I don't go to white churches who still try and push that bullshit rhetoric.

I don't like white Christian songs that sing about, "…wash me and make me whiter than snow…" and other songs that mention the need to be "white and pure like God", so I don't sing any of their songs when I go to a white church. So, for those reasons, I don't like going to white churches. That plus the fact that I'm black and petty.

When I drive down the street and know an old white guy wants to get over in front of me, I used to speed up. Why? I do that because he looks like he is the age of the white men who are responsible for lynching and raping black men, women and children during the period of history before the civil rights movement started.

Another reason is because I don't want to give him shit because he probably called grown-ass black men "boy", wouldn't hire a man for being black, loves black female prostitutes and would deny black men bank loans…and because I'm black and petty.

I wrote a Private Matter topic on being black and petty and put it in this book. Why? Because I wanted to share my views on

American law, religion, politics and other issues from one black man's

perspective...and because sometimes I can be petty.

The Positive Effects of American Slavery

(By a Christian, African American male)

Everything in life has a cause and effect. At face value, some events may seem to be disastrous and overwhelming; but in the end, as a Christian, I know "He has the world in His hands". The situation I would like to look at and give the reader a different outlook on is American slavery.

I am in no ways trying to downplay the disastrous effects slavery had, and has, on American society. I am simply trying to have people look at every situation in life with a positive, Christian perspective.

The word "slavery", particularly in American society, stirs up depictions of horrible, hate-filled, heart-wrenching events from the past and present. That single word has been the line drawn in the sand in so many areas of our lives. That word sparks memories that most of us weren't even a part of; never the less, we take it personally and let the emotions attached to the "memories" limit our capacity to operate on the level that God intended for us.

Those of us who are able to give first-hand accounts of "Jim Crow" inspired, American law policies, seem to seek comfort based on race and in the end cause more division. As Christians we have to be above the fray and let everyone be on notice that no one word or event will have control over our lives unless the word is the Word of God and the event is Jesus Christ shedding his blood on the cross for our sins!!!

For the record, when I say "we" I am not referring to blacks or whites...I am referring to humans. You see, we have to start operating from a position of control and power! As individuals made in the image of God, and as such, we are more than conquerors! We are all fully equipped to handle what life throws our way and no weapon formed against us shall prosper!

Let's get back to the original topic of this paper: The Positive Effects of American Slavery. Remember that as Christians we operate on a different level that the world is not familiar with. With that knowledge we know that God had a plan for slavery. Prior to slavery, black people weren't exactly rushing to get to America. Africans did not see America as a nice place to take a vacation, do business or even put as a destination on their "bucket lists".

I have to say it: without this hot-button issue called slavery, the world as we know it would not be what it is today, for better or for worse. Since God's will trumps our will (or lack of), He decided to use slavery as His method of choice for getting Africans to America.

Our confidence in God's will no matter what it may seem, needs to be unshakeable. *Especially* since Jesus tells us to thank God daily that "His will is done on earth as it is in heaven".

When you look at it from that standpoint, it takes all the blame out the game. It removes all the past pain. It removes all the questioning. It removes all discussions related to "fixing the wrongs of the past".

As Christians, we need to step up and be examples not excuses. Because if we view it from the worldly view that it was such a terrible thing and that it should have never happened and we as humans can somehow "make it right", we may find ourselves in the awkward position that Job was in when he decided to question God and His ways. God let him know in no uncertain terms that he was not, is not and never will be in Any position to question what and why God does what He does.

As Christians we need to be examples to the world on all issues. Through one man the world fell into sin and gave up his position of authority over the earth to Satan, and through one man we conquered sin and regained our position of authority over the earth from Satan.

The Bible says "anyone who begins to plow and look back is not ready to do God's work". Let's stop looking back people. We as humans are not at war with each other, but at war with the real, even though unseen, forces of evil. I am not here to say that the Congressional Black Caucus, Hispanic Movie Awards, and Minority Chambers of Commerce's did not serve a purpose. The very need for their existence exposes the problem with the way things are being done; at the same time, they provide a backdrop for more division amongst people.

So, what can be done? We should prepare for battle from the Biblical standpoint and not concern ourselves with these petty, divisive tactics that the real enemy Satan, not humans, is using. Monitor them from a distance, but not let them taint our views of each other or ourselves. We should begin to do unto others as you would have them do unto you.

This means those who are misusing positions of authority need to look at how they would feel if the same things were being done to them and how God deals with those who misuse the authority he has given them; and this also means that the people who are and have been wronged need to look to God for recourse, not earthly methods of reparations.

God revealed something very interesting to me while I was reading Revelations. Apparently, they had a situation in Heaven where 7 scrolls that contained exquisite revealing powers needed to be opened but no one was qualified to do such a thing. Then an angel said "the blessed Lamb of God can".

What follows next is what really got me: the angel said the Lamb was qualified because he paid the ultimate price so that he could bring people to God and **because he led people of all nations and races into ONE glorious kingdom, to rule the earth!!!!!** If we want to be considered worthy on any level that matters, we need to follow this example set by Jesus and start doing the work of bringing people from all races and nations together into the Kingdom of God so we can get this earth back to the way it needs to be!!!

RANDOM SHIT

Thought: If the Earth is round, why don't people on the bottom half of the Earth fall off? Aren't they technically upside-down? Is the pull of gravity heavier for them?

Saying: "Snitches get stitches." That means if you tell on somebody and they find out...yo' ass is gonna get fucked up and need some stitches.

Saying: "I want some head." It does not mean you are hungry and want a head of lettuce, a head of cabbage or anything to do with a literal head...unless you are talking about a dick head. That's because this saying means you want to get your dick sucked.

Saying: "If you hang with a lame, you'll walk with a limp." That means if you hang with somebody long enough, you will eventually act just like them. This one is literal...but not literal. The word "lame" in this context means "a person who isn't doing shit, a buster, a clown" but it also works in this saying because someone who is literally lame literally walks with a limp.

Thought: The word "fuck" is probably the most versatile word on the planet, second only to "shit." It means sex, as in, "Let's fuck." It's used to emphasis or to stress any point you ever want to make, as in, "I'm serious! Leave me the fuck alone!" It is a noun because it describes a person, as in, "He's a dumb fuck." It describes a direction or can be used as an instruction, as in, "Get the fuck out of here and go *that* fucking way." It fills in any blank you have in a sentence, as in, "I'm mad as fuck

Saying: "He don't believe fat meat is greasy." That means you have a hard time understanding the truth. This saying is usually used when someone doesn't believe they will get fucked up. For example, if your neighbor keeps letting his dog shit in your front yard, even after you've told him that both him and his dog will get fucked up...the truth is that one day, if it keeps happening, they both will get fucked up. Well, one of these days when you've had enough of the bullshit and you fuck both of them up...your neighbor and his dog will understand that you meant what you said. You were telling the truth.

Saying: "I will bust his head open to the white meat!" That means you are angry enough to hit somebody on they head so hard their skull busts open like a coconut; leaving the brain, aka "the white meat", exposed.

Saying: "That's not what I meant" means, "That's *exactly* what I meant."

Thought: If the 1st English immigrants that came to America hadn't wiped out almost every form of wild, carnivorous animal on the North American continent, America would be a scary ass place to be. There would be bears, wolves and mountain lions in our backyards, front yards and alleys. I know I would *never* set the trash out front on the curb at nighttime by myself.

Saying: "It's just a white lie." That means its's still a lie, but it's so politely sneaky and deceptive that you don't really feel like it's a lie.

PERSONAL DEVELOPMENT NOTES

PERSONAL DEVELOPMENT NOTES

PERSONAL DEVELOPMENT NOTES